MODE *at* ROWAN

Pure Cashmere

10 Hand Knit Designs

quail studio

CREDITS

Photography
Quail Studio

Art Direction & Styling
Georgina Brant

Hair & MakeUp
Vanessa - Court-on-Camera Creatives

Design Layout
Quail Studio

Model
Amy Dean

Knitters
Gina Couch • Sheila Player • Lauren Sheilds • Sue Taylor
Victoria Drake • Julie Goodman • Amanda Fowler • Fiona Rollins
Catherine Eastham • Liz Agnew • Rebecca Cox • Hannah Tebbutt
Jane Poore • Margo Brunton • Mim Pitman

First published in Great Britain in 2021 by
Quail Publishing Limited
Unit 15, Green Farm, Fritwell, Bicester, Oxfordshire,
OX27 7QU
e-mail: info@quailstudio.co.uk

Mode Pure Cashmere
ISBN: 978-1-9162445-9-7

MODE

Pure Cashmere

Enjoy the subtle luxury of pure cashmere with this contemporary collection
from MODE. Whether you're enhancing your work-from-home loo or
adding a touch of luxury to your loungewear, feather-light cashmere
provides the ultimate in reassuring warmth and is perfect for layering in
the cooler months. Including undulating cables, cosy ribs and stocking
stitch panels, knitters of all levels will delight in the indulgent sensation of
knitting with this beautiful and timeless yarn.

Pure Cashmere

COLLECTION

10 HAND KNIT DESIGNS

Hartley pattern page 32

Joslyn pattern page 36

Miya pattern page 28

Calla pattern page 38

Fleur pattern page 42

Understated & timeless luxury.

Taylor pattern page 46

Caggie pattern page 48

Dinah pattern page 52

Ina pattern page 54

Shay pattern page 50

Miya

PATTERN PAGE 28

Hartley

PATTERN PAGE 32

Joslyn

PATTERN PAGE 36

Calla

PATTERN PAGE 38

Fleur

PATTERN PAGE 42

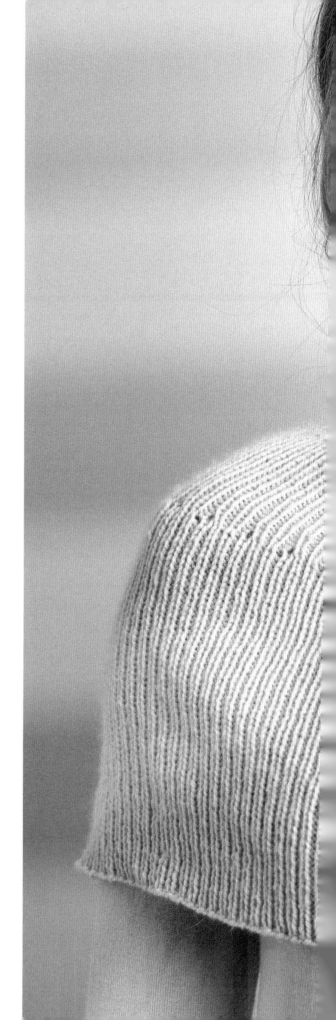

Taylor

PATTERN PAGE 46

Shay

Caggie

PATTERN PAGES 48 & 50

Dinah

PATTERN PAGE 52

Ina

PATTERN PAGE 54

Patterns

Miya

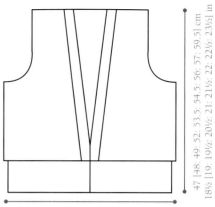

44 [48.5: 53.5: 57: 62.5: 66.5: 72: 76: 81] cm
17¼ [19: 21: 22½: 24½: 26¼: 28¼: 30: 32] in

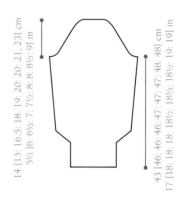

SIZE

To fit bust

71-76	81-86	91-97	102-107	112-117	122-127	132-137	142-147	152-157	cm
28-30	32-34	36-38	40-42	44-46	48-50	52-54	56-58	60-62	in

Actual bust measurement of garment

88	97	107	114	125	133	144	152	162	cm
34.5	38	42	45	49	52.5	56.5	60	64	in

YARN

Pure Cashmere

7	7	7	8	8	9	9	10	10	x 50gm

(photographed in Dawn 92)

NEEDLES

1 pair 4mm (no 8) (US 6) needles

TENSION

23 sts and 32 rows to 10cm/4in measured over P2, K1 Rib using 4mm (US 6) needles

EXTRAS

Stitch holders
Stitch markers
3 buttons

BACK

Using 4mm (US 6) needles, cast on 89 [99: 111: 123: 129: 139: 151: 159: 171] sts.

Row 1 (RS): K1, *P1, K1; rep from * to end.

Row 2 (WS): P1, *K1, P1; rep from * to end.

Last 2 rows set pattern.

Work in rib patt for 8cm, increasing 11 [10: 10: 7: 13: 12: 12: 13: 13] sts evenly spaced across last WS row.
100 [109: 121: 130: 142: 151: 163: 172: 184] sts.

Row 1 (RS): K1, *P2, K1; rep from * to end.

Row 2 (WS): P1, *K2, P1; rep from * to end.

Last 2 rows set pattern.

Work in pattern until back meas 29 [29: 29: 30.5: 30.5: 30.5: 32: 32: 33] cm, ending with a WS row.

Shape armholes

Cast off 3 [4: 5: 6: 8: 8: 10: 10: 12] sts at beg of next 2 rows, 3 sts at beg of the foll 2 [2: 2: 4: 4: 6: 6: 8: 8] rows,
2 sts at beg of foll 4 [4: 6: 4: 6: 6: 6: 6: 8] rows, dec 1 st each side every alt row 4 [5: 6: 6: 6: 6: 8: 8: 8] times.
72 [77: 81: 86: 90: 93: 97: 100: 104] sts.

Cont straight until armhole meas 18 [19: 20: 21.5: 23: 24: 24: 25: 26.5] cm, ending with a WS row.

Cast off all sts.

Pattern note – slip first stitch on opening edge on both fronts throughout

LEFT FRONT

Using 4mm (US 6) needles, cast on 39 [45: 51: 55: 61: 67: 73: 79: 85] sts.

Row 1 (RS): K1, *P1, K1; rep from * to end.

Row 2 (WS): P1, *K1, P1; rep from * to end.

Last 2 rows set pattern.

Cont in rib patt as set for 8cm, increasing 9 [9: 9: 11: 11: 11: 11: 11: 11] sts evenly spaced across last WS row,
but do NOT increase over the first 8 sts. 48 [54: 60: 66: 72: 78: 84: 90: 96] sts.

Next row (RS): K1, * P2, K1; rep from * to last 8 sts, [P1, K1] to end.

Next row (WS): [P1, K1] 4 times, P1, *K2, P1, rep from * to end.

Last 2 rows set pattern.

Cont in patt as set until Left Front meas 12 [12: 13: 16: 16: 16: 18: 19: 21.5] cm, ending with a WS row.

Shape V-neck and armhole

Dec row (RS): Patt last 11 sts, K2tog, K1, [P1, K1] 4 times. 47 [53: 59: 65: 71: 77: 83: 89: 95] sts.

Cont in patt for 13 [9: 9: 7: 7: 5: 5: 5: 5] rows straight.

Rep last 14 [10: 10: 8: 8: 6: 6: 6: 6] rows 6 [9: 9: 11: 12: 15: 15: 18: 18] times more, AT THE SAME TIME, when
Left Front meas 29 [29: 29: 30.5: 30.5: 30.5: 32: 32: 33] cm from beg, ending with RS facing for next row and work
armhole shaping (while cont neck shaping) as foll:

Next row (RS): Cast off 3 [4: 5: 6: 8: 8: 10: 10: 12] sts, patt to end.

Cont to cast off from armhole edge, 3 sts 1 [1: 1: 2: 2: 3: 3: 4: 4] time(s), 2 sts 2 [2: 3: 2: 3: 3: 3: 3: 4] times, dec 1 st
every alt row 4 [5: 6: 6: 6: 6: 8: 8: 8] times. 27 [28: 30: 32: 33: 33: 35: 35: 37] sts.

After all neck and armhole dec's have been worked, cont straight until armhole meas 18 [19: 20: 21.5: 23: 24: 24:
25: 26.5] cm, ending with RS facing for next row.

Next row (RS): Cast off 19 [20: 22: 24: 25: 25: 27: 27: 29] sts for shoulder, patt to end.

Place rem 8 sts on a holder.

Place markers on front ribbed band for 3 buttons, the first one 1.5cm from cast-on edge, the last one 1.5cm from
start of V-neck, and the 3rd one evenly between.

RIGHT FRONT

Using 4mm (US 6) needles, cast on 39 [45: 51: 55: 61: 67: 73: 79: 85] sts.

Row 1 (RS): P1, *K1, P1; rep from * to end.

Row 2 (WS): K1, *P1, K1; rep from * to end.

Last 2 rows set pattern.

Cont in rib pattern for a further 2 rows.

Buttonhole row (RS): Patt 3 sts, cast off 3 sts, patt to end. On foll row, cast on 3 sts over cast-off sts.

Rep buttonhole row twice more, opposite markers on Left Front.

Cont in K1, P1 Rib until 8cm from beg, and inc 9 [9: 9: 11: 11: 11: 11: 11: 11] sts evenly spaced across last WS row, but do NOT decrease over the last 8 sts. 48 [54: 60: 66: 72: 78: 84: 90: 96] sts.

Next row (RS): [K1, P1] 4 times, K1, *P2, K1; rep from * to end.

Next row (WS): *P1, K2; rep from * to last 9 sts, P1, [K1, P1] 4 times.

Last 2 rows set patt.

Cont in patt as set until Right Front meas 12 [12: 13: 16: 16: 16: 18: 19: 21.5] cm, ending with a WS row.

Shape V-neck and armhole

Dec row (RS): [K1, P1] 4 times, K1, SKP, patt to end. 47 [53: 59: 65: 71: 77: 83: 89: 95] sts.

Cont in patt for 13 [9: 9: 7: 7: 5: 5: 5: 5] rows straight.

Rep last 14 [10: 10: 8: 8: 6: 6: 6: 6] rows 6 [9: 9: 11: 12: 15: 15: 18: 18] times more, AT THE SAME TIME, when Right Front meas 29 [29: 29: 30.5: 30.5: 30.5: 32: 32: 33] cm from beg, ending with WS facing for next row and work armhole shaping (while cont neck shaping) as foll:

Next row (WS): Cast off 3 [4: 5: 6: 8: 8: 10: 10: 12] sts, patt to end.

Cont to cast off from armhole edge, 3 sts 1 [1: 1: 2: 2: 3: 3: 4: 4] time(s), 2 sts 2 [2: 3: 2: 3: 3: 3: 3: 4] times, dec 1 st every alt row 4 [5: 6: 6: 6: 6: 8: 8: 8] times. 27 [28: 30: 32: 33: 33: 35: 35: 37] sts.

After all neck and armhole dec's have been worked, cont straight until armhole meas 18 [19: 20: 21.5: 23: 24: 24: 25: 26.5] cm, ending with WS facing for next row.

Next row (WS): Cast off 19 [20: 22: 24: 25: 25: 27: 27: 29] sts for shoulder, patt to end.

Place rem 8 sts on a holder.

SLEEVES

Using 4mm (US 6) needles, cast on 45 [45: 45: 47: 47: 47: 51: 51: 53] sts.

Row 1 (RS): K1, *P1, K1; rep from * to end.

Row 2 (WS): P1, *K1, P1; rep from * to end.

Last 2 rows set pattern.

Work in rib pattern for 10cm, increasing 1 [1: 1: 2: 2: 2: 1: 1: 2] st(s) on last WS row. 46 [46: 46: 49: 49: 49: 52: 52: 55] sts.

Row 1 (RS): K1, *P2, K1; rep from * to end.

Row 2 (WS): P1, *K2, P1; rep from * to end.

Last 2 rows set pattern.

Work in rib and inc 1 st each side (working inc'd sts into patt) every row 6 times, then every foll alt row 7 times. 72 [72: 72: 75: 75: 75: 78: 78: 81] sts.

Cont in rib for 4 [4: 8: 8: 10: 10: 6: 4] rows straight.

Inc 1 st each side on next row. 74 [74: 74: 77: 77: 77: 80: 80: 83] sts.

Work 15 [11: 7: 5: 3: 3: 3: 3: 3] rows straight.

Rep last 16 [12: 8: 6: 4: 4: 4: 4: 4] rows 3 [6: 9: 11: 16: 18: 19: 21: 22] times more. 80 [86: 92: 99: 109: 113: 118: 122: 127] sts.

Cont straight until sleeve meas 43 [46: 46: 46: 47: 47: 47: 48: 48] cm, ending with a WS row.

Shape sleeve head

Cast off 3 [4: 5: 6: 8: 8: 10: 10: 12] sts at beg of next 2 rows, 3 sts at beg of the foll 2 rows, 2 sts at beg of foll 2 [2: 2: 2: 4: 4: 4: 4: 2] rows, dec 1 st each side every alt row 17 [19: 21: 23: 24: 26: 26: 28: 31] times, then cast off 3 sts at beg of foll 4 rows.

Cast off rem 18 [18:18: 19: 19: 19: 20: 20: 19] sts.

MAKING UP

Press as described on information page.

Join shoulder seams.

Neckband

With RS facing and using 4mm (US 6) needle, cont rib across 8 sts on left front holder. Cont in rib until piece fits along one half of back neck. Place sts on holder. Work in same way, using 8 sts from right front holder. Join open sts tog at centre back neck. Sew sides of neckband along cast-off sts of back neck.

Sew in sleeves.

Join side and sleeve seam.

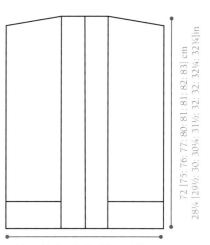

72 [75: 76: 77: 80: 81: 81: 82: 83] cm
28¼ [29½: 30: 30¼: 31½: 32: 32: 32¼: 32¾] in

50 [55: 60: 65: 70: 75: 80: 85: 90] cm
19½ [21½: 23½: 25½: 27½: 29½: 31½: 33½: 35½] in

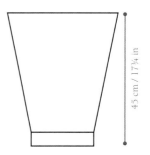

45 cm / 17¾ in

SIZE
To fit bust

71-76	81-86	91-97	102-107	112-117	122-127	132-137	142-147	152-157	cm
28-30	32-34	36-38	40-42	44-46	48-50	52-54	56-58	60-62	in

Actual bust measurement of garment

100	110	120	130	140	150	160	170	180	cm
39	43	47	51	55	59	63	67	71	in

YARN
Pure Cashmere

9	9	10	10	11	11	12	12	13	x 50gm

(photographed in Port 93)

NEEDLES
1 pair each sizes 3.5mm (no 9 / 10) (US 4) and 3.75mm (no 9) (US 5) needles

TENSION
22 sts and 30 rows to 10cm/4in measured over st st using 3.75mm (US 5) needles

EXTRAS
Stitch holders
Stitch markers

BACK

Using 3.5mm (US 4) needles, cast on 115 [123: 135: 147: 159: 169: 181: 193: 205] sts.

Row 1 (RS): *K1, P1; rep from * to last st, K1.

Row 2 (WS): *P1, K1; rep from * to last st, P1.

Last 2 rows set pattern.

Work in rib patt until back meas 8 cm, dec 5 [5: 5: 7: 7: 7: 7: 9: 9] sts evenly spaced across last WS row. 110 [118: 130: 140: 152: 162: 174: 184: 196] sts.

Change to 3.75mm (US 5) needles.

Starting with a K row, work in st st until back meas 48 [50: 50: 50: 51: 51: 51: 51: 51] cm, ending with a WS row.

Place stitch marker each side of row for beg of armholes.

Cont straight until armhole meas 18 [19: 20: 21: 23: 24: 24: 25: 26] cm from markers, ending with a WS row.

Shape shoulders

Cast off 7 [8: 9: 10: 11: 12: 13: 14: 15] sts at beg of next 8 rows and 8 [8: 8: 9: 10: 11: 13: 13: 15] sts at beg of next 2 rows. Cast off rem 38 [38: 42: 42: 44: 44: 44: 46: 46] sts for back neck.

LEFT FRONT

Using 3.5mm (US 4) needles, cast on 49 [53: 59: 63: 69: 73: 79: 83: 89] sts.

Row 1 (RS): *K1, P1; rep from * to last st, K1.

Row 2 (WS): *P1, K1; rep from * to last st, P1.

Last 2 rows set pattern.

Work in rib patt until front meas 8cm and work last WS row as foll:

Next row (WS) Rib 12 sts, rib to end and dec 1 [1: 3: 2: 3: 2: 2: 2: 2] st(s) evenly to end of row. 48 [52: 56: 61: 66: 71: 77: 81: 87] sts.

Change to 3.75mm (US 5) needles.

Next row (RS): Knit to last 12 sts, place marker, [P1, K1] 6 times (for ribbed band).

Next row (WS): Sl 1 st wyif, cont rib to marker, slip marker, purl to end.

Last 2 rows set pattern.

Cont in patt until front meas 48 [50: 50: 50: 51: 51: 51: 51: 51] cm, ending with a WS row.

Place stitch marker at beg of RS row for beg of armholes.

Cont straight until armhole meas 18 [19: 20: 21: 23: 24: 24: 25: 26] cm from markers, ending with a WS row.

Shape shoulders

Next row (RS): Cast off 7 [8: 9: 10: 11: 12: 13: 14: 15] sts (shoulder edge), patt to end. 41 [44: 47: 51: 55: 59: 64: 67: 72] sts.

Cont to cast off 7 [8: 9: 10: 11: 12: 13: 14: 15] sts from shoulder edge 3 times more, then 8 [8: 8: 9: 10: 11: 13: 13: 15] sts once. Place rem 12 sts on a holder.

RIGHT FRONT

Using 3.5mm (US 4) needles, cast on 49 [53: 59: 63: 69: 73: 79: 83: 89] sts.

Row 1 (RS): *K1, P1; rep from * to last st, K1.

Row 2 (WS): *P1, K1; rep from * to last st, P1.

Last 2 rows set pattern.

Work in rib patt until front meas 8cm and work last WS row as foll:

Next row (WS) Rib to last 12 sts dec 1 [1: 3: 2: 3: 2: 2: 2: 2] st(s) evenly, then rib last 12 sts. 48 [52: 56: 61: 66: 71: 77: 81: 87] sts.

Change to 3.75mm (US 5) needles.

Next row (RS): Sl 1 st wyib. P1, [K1, P1] 5 times (for ribbed band), place marker, knit to end.

Next row (WS): Purl to marker, slip marker, [K1, P1] 6 times.

Last 2 rows set pattern.

Cont in patt until front meas 48 [50: 50: 50: 51: 51: 51: 51: 51] cm, ending with a WS row.

Place stitch marker at end of RS row for beg of armholes.

Cont straight until armhole meas 18 [19: 20: 21: 23: 24: 24: 25: 26] cm from markers, ending with a RS row.

Shape shoulders

Next row (WS): Cast off 7 [8: 9: 10: 11: 12: 13: 14: 15] sts (shoulder edge), patt to end. 41 [44: 47: 51: 55: 59: 64: 67: 72] sts.

Cont to cast off 7 [8: 9: 10: 11: 12: 13: 14: 15] sts from shoulder edge 3 times more, then 8 [8: 8: 9: 10: 11: 13: 13: 15] sts once. Place rem 12 sts on a holder.

SLEEVES

Using 3.5mm (US 4) needles, cast on 47 [49: 49: 49: 53: 53: 53: 55: 55] sts.

Row 1 (RS): *K1, P1; rep from * to last st, K1.

Row 2 (WS): *P1, K1; rep from * to last st, P1.

Last 2 rows set pattern.

Work in rib patt until sleeve meas 5cm, ending with a WS row.

Change to 3.75mm (US 5) needles.

Starting with a K row, work in st st for 6 rows.

Inc 1 st each side on next row. 49 [51: 51: 51: 55: 55: 55: 57: 57] sts.

Cont to inc 1 st each side every foll 6th row 11 [11: 15: 11: 9: 3: 3: 0: 12] times more, then every foll 8th [8th: 4th: 4th: 4th: 4th: 4th: 4th: 2nd] row 5 [5: 4: 10: 13: 22: 22: 27: 17] times. 81 [83: 89: 93: 99: 105: 105: 111: 115] sts.

Cont straight until sleeve meas 45cm, ending with a WS row.

Cast off all sts loosely.

MAKING UP

Press as described on information page.

Join both shoulder seams.

Neckband

With RS facing and using 3.75mm (US 5) needles, cont rib across 12 sts on left front holder. Cont in rib until piece fits along one half of back neck. Place sts on holder. Work in same way, using 12 sts from right front holder. Join open sts tog at centre back neck. Sew sides of neckband along cast-off sts of back neck.

Sew in sleeves.

Join side and sleeve seams.

Joslyn

SIZE
To fit an average-sized adult woman's head
Actual circumference 48cm/19in

YARN
Pure Cashmere
     1   x 50gm
(photographed in Potash 99)

NEEDLES
1 pair size 3.5mm (no 9/10) (US 4) needles

TENSION
23 sts and 34 rows to 10cm/4in measured over K1, P1 Rib using 3.5mm (US 4) when slightly stretched

SPECIAL ABBREVIATIONS
S2KP: Slip 2 sts tog knitwise as if to K2tog, K1, pass 2 slipped sts over K1. 2 sts dec'd

HAT

Using 3.5mm (US 4) needles, cast on 111 sts.
Row 1 (RS): K1, *P1, K1; rep from * to end.
Row 2 (WS): P1, *K1, P1; rep from * to end.
Last 2 rows set pattern.
Work in rib patt for 18cm, ending with a WS row.
Shape top
Row 1 (RS): K1, [P1, S2KP, rib 18] 5 times. 101 sts.
Row 2 and all WS rows: Work in patt.
Row 3: K1, [P1, S2KP, rib 16] 5 times. 91 sts.
Row 5: K1, [P1, S2KP, rib 14] 5 times. 81 sts.
Row 7: K1, [P1, S2KP, rib 12] 5 times. 71 sts.
Row 9: K1, [P1, S2KP, rib 10] 5 times. 61 sts.
Row 11: K1, [P1, S2KP, rib 8] 5 times. 51 sts.
Row 13: K1, [P1, S2KP, rib 6] 5 times. 41 sts.
Row 15: K1, [P1, S2KP, rib 4] 5 times. 31 sts.
Row 17: K1, [S2KP] 10 times. 11 sts.

MAKING UP

Cut yarn, leaving enough for sewing up.
Pull yarn through rem sts and pull to secure. Sew back seam.

Calla

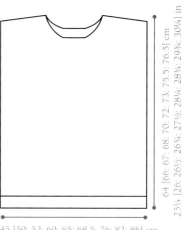

64 [66: 67: 68: 70: 72: 73: 75.5: 76.5] cm
25¼ [26: 26½: 26¾: 27½: 28¼: 28¾: 29¾: 30¾] in

45 [50: 53: 60: 65: 68.5: 76: 82: 86] cm
17¾ [19½: 21: 23¾: 25½: 27: 29¾. 32¼. 34] in

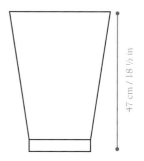

47 cm / 18 ½ in

SIZE
To fit bust

71-76	81-86	91-97	102-107	112-117	122-127	132-137	142-147	152-157	cm
28-30	32-34	36-38	40-42	44-46	48-50	52-54	56-58	60-62	in

Actual bust measurement of garment

90	100	106	120	130	137	152	164	172	cm
35.5	39	42	47.5	51	54	59.5	64.5	68	in

YARN
Pure Cashmere

10	11	11	12	12	13	13	14	15	x 50gm

(photographed in Light 15)

NEEDLES
1 pair each sizes 3.5mm (no 9/10) (US 4) and 3.75mm (no 9) (US 5) needles
1 x 3.5mm (no 9/10) (US 4) circular needle

TENSION
28 sts and 30 rows to 10 cm/4 in measured over cable pattern using 3.75mm (US 5) needles

EXTRAS
Cable needle
Stitch markers

Note: st st rows at the lower hem and sleeve cuff edges are not included in the finished length measurements or shown on the schematics.

BACK

Using 3.5mm (US 4) needles, cast on 103 [113: 121: 137: 147: 155: 171: 185: 195] sts.

Starting with a K row, work in st st for 8 rows.

Row 1 (RS): K1, *P1, K1; rep from * to end.

Row 2 (WS): P1, *K1, P1; rep from * to end.

Last 2 rows set pattern.

Work in rib patt for 4cm, increasing 21 [23: 27: 29: 31: 35: 37: 41: 43] sts evenly spaced across last WS row. 124 [136: 148: 166: 178: 190: 208: 226: 238] sts.

Change to 3.75mm (US 5) needles

Row 1 (RS): Knit.

Row 2 and every alt row (WS): Purl.

Row 3: K1, *K2, slip 2 sts to cn and hold to *back*, K2, K2 from cn (C4B); rep from * to last 3 sts, k3.

Row 5: Knit.

Row 7: K1, *slip 2 sts to cn and hold to *front*, K2, K2 from cn (C4F), K2; rep from * to last 3 sts, k3.

Row 8: Purl.

These 8 rows set pattern.

Repeat last 8 rows until back meas 43 [44: 44: 44: 45: 45: 45: 46: 46] cm, ending with a WS row.

Place stitch marker each side of row for beg of armholes.

Cont in patt until armhole meas 17 [18: 19: 20: 21: 23: 24: 25.5: 26.5] cm, ending with a WS row.

Mark the centre 40 [42: 44: 46: 48: 48: 50: 50: 52] sts.

Shape shoulders and neck

Cast off 12 [15: 16: 18: 21: 23: 25: 28: 29] sts, work to the centre marked sts, turn, leaving rem sts on holder. 30 [32: 36: 42: 44: 48: 54: 60: 64] sts.

Work each side separately.

Next row (WS): Cast off 2 sts (neck edge), patt to end. 28 [30: 34: 40: 42: 46: 52: 58: 62] sts.

Cont to cast off at shoulder edge 13 [14: 16: 19: 20: 22: 25: 28: 30] sts twice, AND AT SAME TIME, cast off from neck edge 2 sts once more.

With RS facing, rejoin yarn to rem 82 [89: 96: 106: 113: 119: 129: 138: 145] sts, cast off 40 [42: 44: 46: 48: 48: 50: 50: 52] sts, and patt to end. 42 [47: 52: 60: 65: 71: 79: 88: 93] sts.

Complete to match first side, reversing shapings.

FRONT

Work as for Back until armholes meas 13 [14: 15: 16: 17: 19: 20: 21.5: 22.5] cm, ending with a WS row.

Shape neck and shoulders

Next row (RS): K48 [53: 58: 66: 71: 77: 85: 94: 99] sts, turn, leaving rem sts on holder. Work each side separately.

Next row (WS): Cast off 3 sts (neck edge), patt to end. 45 [50: 55: 63: 68: 74: 82: 91: 96] sts.

Cont to cast off 2 sts from neck edge once, then dec 1 st at neck edge every alt row 5 times; AT SAME TIME, when armhole measures same length as back to shoulder, shape shoulder by casting off 12 [15: 16: 18: 21: 23: 25: 28: 29] sts once, 13 [14: 16: 19: 20: 22: 25: 28: 30] sts twice.

With RS facing, rejoin yarn to rem 76 [83: 90: 100: 107: 113: 123: 132: 139] sts, cast off 28 [30: 32: 34: 36: 36: 38: 38: 40] sts, and patt to end. 48 [53: 58: 66: 71: 77: 85: 94: 99] sts.

Complete to match first side, reversing shapings.

SLEEVES

Using 3.5mm (US 4) needles, cast on 47 [47: 47: 51: 51: 51: 51: 57: 57] sts.

Starting with a K row, work in st st for 8 rows.

Row 1 (RS): K1, *P1, K1; rep from * to end.

Row 2 (WS): P1, *K1, P1; rep from * to end.

Last 2 rows set pattern.

Work in rib patt for 4cm, increasing 11 [11: 11: 13: 13: 13: 13: 13: 13] sts evenly spaced across last WS row. 58 [58: 58: 64: 64: 64: 64: 70: 70] sts.

Change to 3.75mm (US 5) needles.

Working cable pattern as set for Back and taking increased sts into pattern, increase 1 st st each end of next and every foll 6th [4th: 4th: 4th: 4th: 2nd: 2nd: 2nd: 2nd] row 14 [2: 14: 14: 26: 4: 12: 12: 20] times more, then every foll 8th [6th: 6th: 6th: 6th: 4th: 4th: 4th: 4th] row 3 [17: 9: 9: 1: 26: 22: 22: 18] times.

94 [98: 106: 112: 120: 126: 134: 140: 148] sts.

Cont straight until sleeve meas 47cm, ending with a WS row.

Cast off all sts loosely.

MAKING UP

Press as described on information page.

Join shoulder seams.

Neckband

With RS facing and using 3.5mm (US 4) circular needle, beg at back neck, pick up and knit 5 sts along shaped edge, 40 [42: 44: 46: 48: 48: 50: 50: 52] sts along cast-off back neck sts, pick up and knit 5 sts along shaped back neck edge, 14 sts along shaped front neck edge, 28 [30: 32: 34: 36: 36: 38: 38: 40] sts along cast-off front neck sts, 14 sts along shaped front neck edge. 106 [110: 114: 118: 122: 122: 126: 126: 130] sts. Join and place marker for beg of rnd.

Rnd 1: *K1, P1; rep from * around.

This rnd forms rib.

Rep last rnd until neckband meas 6cm.

Cast off sts loosely in rib.

Sew in sleeves.

Join side and sleeve seams.

Fleur

∷∷○○
∷∷○○

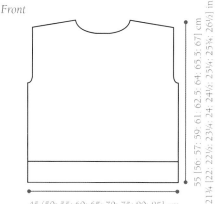

Front

55 [56: 57: 59: 61: 62.5: 64: 65.5: 67] cm
21¾ [22: 22½: 23¼: 24: 24½: 25¼: 25¾: 26½] in

45 (50: 55: 60: 65: 70: 75: 80: 85] cm
17½ (19½: 21½: 23½: 25½: 27½: 29½: 31½: 33½] in

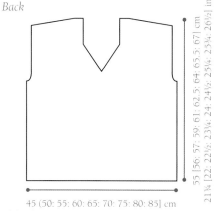

Back

55 [56: 57: 59: 61: 62.5: 64: 65.5: 67] cm
21¾ [22: 22½: 23¼: 24: 24½: 25¼: 25¾: 26½] in

45 (50: 55: 60: 65: 70: 75: 80: 85] cm
17½ (19½: 21½: 23½: 25½: 27½: 29½: 31½: 33½] in

SIZE

To fit bust

71-76	81-86	91-97	102-107	112-117	122-127	132-137	142-147	152-157	cm
28-30	32-34	36-38	40-42	44-46	48-50	52-54	56-58	60-62	in

Actual bust measurement of garment

90	100	110	120	130	140	150	160	170	cm
35	39	43	47	51	55	59	63	67	in

YARN

Pure Cashmere

5	5	6	6	7	7	8	8	9	x 50gm

(photographed in Flannel 100)

NEEDLES

1 pair each 3.5mm (no 9/10) (US 4) and 3.75mm (no 9) (US 5) needles
1 each 3.5mm (no 9/10) (US 4) and 3.75mm (no 9) (US 5) circular needle
1 size 3.75mm (no 9) (US 5) double-pointed needle for I-cord cast-off

TENSION

22 sts and 30 rows to 10cm/4 in measured over st st using 3.75mm (US 5) needles

EXTRAS

Stitch holders

FRONT

Using 3.5mm (US 4) needles, cast on 101 [113: 123: 135: 147: 159: 169: 181: 193] sts.

Row 1 (RS): K1, *P1, K1; rep from * to end.

Row 2 (WS): P1, *K1, P1; rep from * to end.

Last 2 rows set pattern.

Work in rib patt for 6cm, decreasing 4 [4: 4: 6: 6: 8: 6: 8: 8] sts evenly spaced across last WS row. 97 [109: 119: 129: 141: 151: 163: 173: 185] sts.

Change to 3.75mm (US 5) needles.

Starting with a K row, work in st st until front meas 33 [33: 33: 34: 34: 34: 35: 35: 35] cm, ending with a WS row.

Shape armholes

Dec 1 st each side on next row, then foll alt row 1 [1: 2: 2: 2: 3: 3: 4: 5] time(s) more. 93 [105: 113: 123: 135: 143: 155: 163: 173] sts.

Cont straight until armhole meas 16 [17: 18: 19: 21: 22: 23: 24.5: 26] cm, ending with a WS row.

Shape neck and shoulders

Next row (RS): Work 35 [41: 44: 47: 52: 55: 61: 65: 70] sts, turn, leaving rem sts on holder.

Work each side separately.

Next row (WS): Cast off 2 sts (neck edge), patt to end. 33 [39: 42: 45: 50: 53: 59: 63: 68] sts.

Cont to cast off 2 sts at neck edge every alt row 3 times more, AND AT SAME TIME, after 6 rows have been worked in neck shaping, cast off at shoulder edge (beg of RS rows) 9 [11: 12: 13: 14: 15: 17: 19: 20] sts once, and 9 [11: 12: 13: 15: 16: 18: 19: 21] twice.

With RS facing, rejoin yarn to rem 58 [64: 69: 76: 83: 88: 94: 98: 103] sts, cast off 23 [23: 25: 29: 31: 33: 33: 33: 33] sts, and patt to end. 35 [41: 44: 47: 52: 55: 61: 65: 70] sts.

Complete to match first side, reversing shapings.

BACK

Work as for Front until armholes meas 3 [3: 4: 4: 5: 5: 5: 6: 6] cm, ending with a WS row.

Shape neck and shoulders

Next row (RS): K 46 [52: 56: 61: 67: 71: 77: 81: 86] sts, turn, leaving rem sts on holder. Work each side separately. Patt 1 row.

Next row (RS): Patt to last 3 sts, k2tog (neck edge), K1. 45 [51: 55: 60: 66: 70: 76: 80: 85] sts.

Cont to dec 1 st at neck edge every alt row 8 [8: 9: 9: 12: 9: 9: 9: 9] times more, then *every* row 6 [6: 6: 8: 4: 8: 8: 8: 8] times. 31 [37: 40: 43: 50: 53: 59: 63: 68] sts.

Work straight in patt until armhole meas 18 [19: 20: 21: 23: 24.5: 25: 26.5: 28] cm, ending with RS facing for the next row.

Shape shoulder

Cast off 9 [11: 12: 13: 14: 15: 17: 19: 20] sts at beg of next RS row, and every alt row 9 [11: 12: 13: 15: 16: 18: 19: 21] sts twice. Place rem 4 [4: 4: 4: 6: 6: 6: 6: 6] sts on a holder.

With RS facing, rejoin yarn to rem 47 [53: 57: 62: 68: 72: 78: 82: 87] sts, K2tog and patt to end. 46 [52: 56: 61: 67: 71: 77: 80: 86] sts.

Complete to match first side, reversing shapings.

MAKING UP

Press as described on information page.

Join shoulder seams using back stitch, or mattress stitch if preferred.

Roll neckband

With RS facing and using 3.5mm (US 4) circular needle, beg at back neck, K 4 [4: 4: 4: 6: 6: 6: 6: 6] sts from holder, cast on 45 [45: 47: 47: 45: 47: 47: 47: 47] sts, K 4 [4: 4: 4: 6: 6: 6: 6: 6] sts from holder, pick up and knit 12 sts along shaped front neck edge, 23 [23: 25: 29: 31: 33: 33: 33: 33] sts along cast-off front neck sts, 12 sts along shaped front neck edge. 100 [100: 104: 108: 112: 116: 116: 116: 116] sts. Join and place marker for beg of rnd.

Rnd 1: *K1, P1; rep from * around.

This rnd forms rib.

Rep last rnd until neckband meas 16cm, ending with a WS row.

Cast off sts loosely in rib. Fold band in half to WS and sew in place.

Armhole border

With RS facing using 3.75mm (US 5) circular needle, pick up and knit 82 [86: 90: 96: 104: 112: 116: 120: 126] sts evenly around one armhole edge, cast on an extra 3 sts. 85 [89: 93: 99: 107: 115: 119: 123: 129] sts.

Next row (RS): With dpn, *K2, K2tog tbl, slide these 3 sts back onto the left needle. Repeat from * until all sts have been worked from circular needle.

Bind off rem 3 sts knitwise.

Work in same way along other armhole edge.

Sew side seams.

Taylor

SIZE

To fit bust

71-97	102-127	132-157	cm
28-38	40-50	52-62	in

Actual circumference of garment at hem

117	143.5	172	cm
46	56½	67¾	in

YARN

Pure Cashmere

3	4	5	x 50gm

(photographed in Light 95)

NEEDLES

1 each 3.5mm (no 9/10) (US 4) circular needles 40cm and 80cm long

TENSION

23 sts and 34 rows to 10cm/4in measured over K1, P1 rib using 3.5mm (US 4) needles when slightly stretched

EXTRA

Stitch marker

SPECIAL ABBREVIATIONS

Dbl inc = lift the horizontal loop between the last worked st on the RH needle and the next st on the
LH needle and place it on the LH needle. Kfb into this loop (2 new sts inc'd).

Pattern note: the cape is knitted in the round from the neck down. Start knitting with the shorter circular needle
for the collar and change to longer circular needle as the number of stitches increases.

CAPE

Using shorter 3.5mm (US 4) circular needle, cast on 108 [132: 144] sts.
Taking care not to twist cast-on edge, place a stitch marker to note beg of round, and join work in round.
Rnds 1 – 6: Knit
Next rnd: * K1, P1; rep from * to end.
Rep last rnd 17 times more.
Next rnd (inc rnd): * K1, P1, (K1, P1, dbl inc) twcie, rep from * to end. 180 [220: 240] sts.
Next rnd: * K1, P1; rep from * to end.
Rep last rnd 33 [39: 39] times more.
Next rnd (inc rnd): * (K1, P1) twice, dbl inc, rep from * to end. 270 [330: 360] sts.
Size 132-157cm/52-62in ONLY.
Next rnd: * K1, P1; rep from * to end.
Rep last rnd 9 times more.
Next rnd (inc rnd): * (K1, P1) 10 times, dbl inc, rep from * to end. 396 sts.
All sizes
Continue working in K1, P1 rib without shaping until work meas 30 [36: 40] cm from first inc round.
Cast off loosely in pattern.

MAKING UP

Press as described on information page.

Caggie

SIZE
Finished wrap meas 41cm (16¼in) wide and 160cm (63in) long.

YARN
Pure Cashmere
A Light 95
    2   x 50gm
B Chalk 94
    5   x 50gm

NEEDLES
1 pair size 3.75mm (no 9) (US 5) needles

TENSION
22 sts and 30 rows to 10cm/4in measured over st st using 3.75mm (US 5) when slightly stretched

Note: Wind two equal balls of colour A for borders. When changing colours, twist yarns on WS to prevent holes in work.

WRAP

Using 3.75mm (US 5) needles, with 1 ball A, cast on 12 sts, join B and cast on 66 sts, join 2nd ball A and cast on 12 sts. 90 sts.

Row 1 (RS): (K1, P1) 6 times, K66 sts, (K1, P1) 6 times.

Row 2: (P1, K1) 6 times, P66 sts, (P1, K1) 6 times.

Cont in patt as set for 160cm, ending with a WS row.

Cast off sts in patt with matching colours.

Shay

SIZE

To fit an average-sized adult woman's head. Completed hat circumference 50cm/20in.

YARN

Rowan Pure Cashmere

     1   x 50gm

(photographed in Light 095)

NEEDLES

1 pair 3.75mm (no 9) (US 5) needles

Set of 4 double-pointed 3.75mm (no 9) (US 5) needles

TENSION

22 sts and 30 rows to 10cm/4in measured over st st, using 3.75mm (US 5) needles

HAT - Working Flat

Using straight 3.75mm (US 5) needles, cast on 110 sts.

Row 1 (RS): Knit.

Row 2: Purl.

Rep last 2 rows until work meas 21cm, ending with a WS row.

Shape Crown

Row 1 (RS): K5, *K2tog, K9 rep from * to last 6 sts, K2tog, K4. 100 sts.

Row 2 and every foll alt row: Purl.

Row 3: K4, * K2tog, K8, rep from * to last 6 sts, K2tog, K4. 90 sts.

Row 5: K4, * K2tog, K7, rep from * to last 5 sts, K2tog, K3. 80 sts.

Row 7: K3, * K2tog, K6, rep from * to last 5 sts, K2tog, K3. 70 sts.

Row 9: K3, * K2tog, K5, rep from * to last 4 sts, K2tog, K2. 60 sts.

Row 11: K2, * K2tog, K4, rep from * to last 4 sts, K2tog, K2. 50 sts.

Row 13: K2, * K2tog, K3, rep from * to last 3 sts, K2tog, K1. 40 sts.

Row 15: K1, * K2tog, K2, rep from * to last 3 sts, K2tog, K1. 30 sts.

Row 17: K1, *K2tog, K1, rep from * to last 2 sts, K2tog. 20 sts.

Row 19: K2tog to end. 10 sts

Cut yarn and thread through rem 10 sts.

Pull tight and fasten off securely.

MAKING UP

Press as described on the information page.

Using mattress stitch, join back seam.

HAT - Working In The Round

Using double-pointed 3.75mm (US 5) needles, cast on 110 sts.

Distribute sts evenly over 3 of the 4 needles and, using the 4th needle and taking care not to twist cast-on edge, work in rounds as follows:

Round 1 (RS). Knit.

Rep last round until work meas 23cm.

Shape Crown

Round 1: K5, * K2tog, K9, rep from * to last 4 sts, K2tog, K4. 100 sts.

Round 2 and every foll alt round: Knit.

Round 3: K4, * K2tog, K8, rep from * to last 4 sts, K2tog, K4. 90 sts.

Round 5: K4, * K2tog, K7, rep from * K2tog, K3. 80 sts.

Round 7: K3, * K2tog, K6, rep from * to last 5 sts, K2tog, K3. 70 sts

Round 9: K3, * K2tog, K5, rep from * to last 4 sts, K2tog, K2. 60 sts.

Round 11: K2, * K2tog, K4, rep from * to last 4 sts, K2tog, K2. 50 sts.

Round 13: K2, * K2tog, K3, rep from * to last 3 sts, K2tog, K1. 40 sts.

Round 15: K1, * K2tog, K2, rep from * to last 3 sts, K2tog, K1. 30 sts.

Round 17: K1, * K2tog, K1, rep from * to last 2 sts, K2tog. 20 sts.

Round 19: K2tog to end. 10 sts.

Cut yarn and thread through rem 10 sts.

Pull tight and fasten off securely.

MAKING UP

Press as described on the information page.

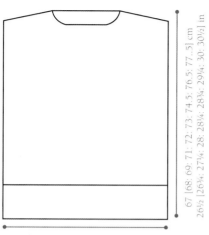

67 [68: 69: 71: 72: 73: 74.5: 76.5: 77.5] cm
26½ [26¾: 27¼: 28: 28¼: 28¾: 29¼: 30: 30½] in

50 [55: 60: 65: 70: 75: 80: 85: 90] cm
19½ [21½: 23½: 25½: 27½: 29½: 31½: 33½: 35½] in

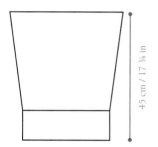

45 cm / 17 ¾ in

Dinah

SIZE
To fit bust

71-76	81-86	91-97	102-107	112-117	122-127	132-137	142-147	152-157	cm
28-30	32-34	36-38	40-42	44-46	48-50	52-54	56-58	60-62	in

Actual bust measurement of garment

100	110	120	130	140	150	160	170	180	cm
39	43	47	51	55	59	63	67	71	in

YARN
Pure Cashmere

9	10	10	11	12	13	13	14	15	x 50gm

(photographed in Potash 99)

NEEDLES
1 pair 3.75mm (no 9) (US 5) needles
1 x 3.75mm (no 9) (US 5) circular needle

TENSION
22 sts and 30 rows to 10cm/4in measured over st st using 3.75mm (US 5) needles

EXTRAS
Stitch holders
Stitch markers

BACK

Using 3.75mm (US 5) needles, cast on 98 [108: 118: 128: 138: 148: 158: 168: 178] sts.

Row 1 (RS): *K3, P2; rep from * to last 3 sts, K3.

Row 2 (WS): *P3, K2; rep from * to last 3 sts, P3.

These 2 rows set pattern.

Work in rib pattern until back meas 10cm increasing 10 [10: 12: 12: 14: 14: 16: 16: 18] sts evenly spaced across last WS row. 108 [118: 130: 140: 152: 162: 174: 184: 196] sts.

Starting with a K row, work in st st until back meas 42 [42: 42: 43: 43: 43: 43.5: 44.5: 44.5] cm, ending with a WS row. Place stitch marker each side of row for beg of armholes.

Cont straight until armhole meas 19 [20: 21: 22: 23: 24: 25: 26: 27] cm from markers, ending with a WS row.

Shape shoulders

Cast off 6 [7: 8: 9: 10: 11: 12: 13: 14] sts at beg of next 8 rows and 7 [8: 9: 10: 11: 12: 13: 14: 16] sts at beg of the foll 2 rows. Place rem 46 [46: 48: 48: 50: 50: 52: 52: 52] sts on a holder for back neck.

FRONT

Work as for Back until armholes meas 18 [19: 20: 21: 22: 23: 24: 25: 26] cm from beg (or 2 rows less than Back to beg of shoulder shaping), ending with a WS row.

Shape neck and shoulders

Next row (RS): K37 [42: 47: 52: 57: 62: 67: 72: 78] sts, turn, leaving rem sts on holder. Work each side separately. Work straight for 1 row.

Next row (RS): Cast off 6 [7: 8: 9: 10: 11: 12: 13: 14] sts, patt to end. 31 [35: 39: 43: 47: 51: 55: 59: 64] sts.

Next row (WS): Cast off 2 sts, patt to end. 29 [33: 37: 41: 45: 49: 53: 57: 62] sts.

Repeat these last 2 rows twice more. 13 [15: 17: 19: 21: 23: 25: 27: 30] sts.

Next row (RS): Cast off 6 [7: 8: 9: 10: 11: 12: 13: 14] sts, patt to end.

Work straight for 1 row.

Cast off rem 7 [8: 9: 10: 11: 12: 13: 14: 16] sts.

With RS facing, place centre 34 [34: 36: 36: 38: 38: 40: 40: 40] sts on a st holder, rejoin yarn to rem 37 [42: 47: 52: 57: 62: 67: 72: 78] sts and patt to end.

Complete to match first side, reversing shapings.

SLEEVES

Using 3.75mm (US 5) needles, cast on on 58 [63: 63: 63: 68: 68: 68: 73: 73] sts.

Row 1 (RS): *K3, P2; rep from * to last 3 sts, K3.

Row 2 (WS): *P3, K2; rep from * to last 3 sts, P3.

These 2 rows set pattern.

Work in rib pattern until sleeve meas 10cm, increasing 6 [7: 7: 7: 8: 8: 8: 7: 7] sts evenly spaced across last WS row. 64 [70: 70: 70: 76: 76: 76: 80: 80] sts.

Starting with a K row work in st st inc 1 st at each end of 9th [9th: 3rd: 9th: 3rd: 9th: 3rd: 3rd: 9th] row, then on every foll 10th [10th: 8th: 6th: 8th: 6th: 6th: 6th: 4th] row to 82 [88: 94: 96: 100: 104: 108: 112: 116] sts.

Cont straight until sleeve meas 45cm ending with a WS row.

Cast off all sts loosely.

MAKING UP

Block as described on information page.

Join shoulder seams using back stitch, or mattress stitch if preferred.

Neckband

With RS facing and using 3.75mm (US 5) circular needle, beg at back neck, knit 46 [46: 48: 48: 50: 50: 52: 52: 52] sts from back neck holder, pick up and knit 10 [10: 11: 11: 11: 11: 11: 11: 11] sts along left front neck, knit 34 [34: 36: 36: 38: 38: 40: 40: 40] sts from front neck holder, pick up and knit 10 [10: 10: 10: 11: 11: 12: 12: 12] sts along right front neck. 100 [100: 105: 105: 110: 110: 115: 115: 115] sts. Join and place marker for beg of rnd.

Rnd 1: *P3, K2; rep from * around.

This rnd forms rib.

Note: RS of rib will show when neckband is folded to the outside.

Rep last rnd until neckband meas 22cm/8.75in.

Cast off sts loosely in rib.

Sew top of sleeve to front and back between armhole markers. Sew sleeve seams. Sew side seams, leaving 10cm/4in of rib at lower edge unsewn for side slits.

Ina

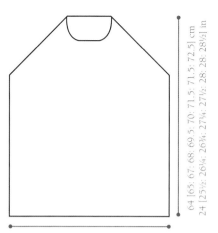

50 [53: 58: 61.5: 66.5: 72.5: 75.5: 80.5: 85.5] cm
19¾ [21: 22¾: 24¼: 26¼: 28¼: 29¾: 31¾: 33¾] in

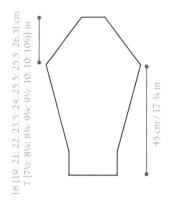

SIZE
To fit bust

71-76	81-86	91-97	102-107	112-117	122-127	132-137	142-147	152-157	cm
28-30	32-34	36-38	40-42	44-46	48-50	52-54	56-58	60-62	cm

Actual bust measurement of garment

100	106	116	123	133	145	151	161	171	cm
39.5	42	45.5	48.5	52.5	56.5	59.5	63.5	67.5	in

YARN
Pure Cashmere

12	12	13	13	14	14	15	15	16	x 50gm

(photographed in Light 95)

NEEDLES
1 pair 3.5mm (no 9 / 10) (US 4) needles
1 size 3.5mm (no 9 / 10) (US 4) circular needle

TENSION
32 sts and 32 rows to 10cm/4in measured over K2, P2 Rib using 3.5mm (US 4) needles, when very slightly stretched
28 sts and 34 rows to 10cm/4in measured over stocking st using 3.5mm (US 4) needles

EXTRAS
Stitch holders
Stitch markers

SPECIAL ABBREVIATIONS

Make One Knit (M1K): With the needle tip, lift the strand between the last stitch worked and the next stitch on left-hand needle and knit it—1 knit stitch increased.

Make One Purl (M1P): With the needle tip, lift the strand between the last stitch worked and the next stitch on left-hand needle and purl it—1 purl stitch increased.

SKP: Slip 1 st, K1, pass slipped st over K1—1 st decreased.

SPP: Slip 1 st, P1, pass the slipped st over P1—1 st decreased.

SK2P: Slip 1, K2tog, pass the slipped st over K2tog—2 sts decreased.

BACK

Using 3.5mm (US 4) needles, cast on 158 [170: 182: 194: 210: 226: 238: 254: 270] sts.

Row 1 (RS): K2, *P2, K2; rep from * to end.

Row 2 (WS): P2, *K2, P2; rep from * to end.

Last 2 rows set pattern.

Work in rib pattern for 46cm, ending with RS facing for next row.

Shape raglan armholes

For first 4 sizes

Dec row 1 (RS): [K2, P2] 3 times, SKP, patt to last 14 sts, K2tog, [P2, K2] 3 times—2 sts dec'd.

Dec row 2 (WS): [P2, K2] 3 times, P2tog, patt to last 14 sts, SPP, [K2, P2] 3 times—2 sts dec'd.

Rep these 2 rows 15 [17: 20: 22] times more. 94 [98: 98: 102] sts.

For last 5 sizes only

Dec row 1 (RS): [K2, P2] 3 times, SK2P, patt to last 15 sts, K3tog, [P2, K2] 3 times—4 sts dec'd.

Dec row 2 (WS): [P2, K2] 3 times, P2tog, patt to last 14 sts, SPP, [K2, P2] 3 times—2 sts dec'd.

Rep these 2 rows 3 [8: 10: 17: 20] times more. [186: 172: 172: 146: 144] sts.

Rep dec rows 1 and 2 same as for first 4 sizes [21:17:17:10: 9] times—[102: 104: 104: 106: 108] sts.

Note: Neck and armhole shaping are worked at the same time. Keep careful track of decreases.

For all sizes—Shape neck

Mark the centre 24 [28: 28: 32: 32: 34: 34: 36: 38] sts.

Next row (RS): [K2, P2] 3 times, SKP, patt to centre marked sts, turn, leaving rem sts on holder. 34 sts.

Work each side separately.

Next row (WS): Patt to last 14 sts, SPP, [K2, P2] 3 times. 33 sts.

Next row: [K2, P2] 3 times, SKP, patt to end. 32 sts.

Next row: Cast off 2 sts (neck dec), patt to to last 14 sts, SPP, [K2, P2] 3 times. 29 sts.

Note: When there are no longer enough sts, work the armhole dec after the 12-st rib band, cont the armhole dec over the last 2 sts of the ribbed band, keeping the rib in place at the armhole edge.

Cont to dec at armhole edge as set 20 times more AND cast off 2 sts from neck edge once more, then dec 1 st at neck edge every alt row 7 times. After all decs have been worked, all sts have been decreased.

With RS facing, rejoin yarn to rem 59 [63: 63: 67: 67: 69: 69: 71: 73] sts, cast off 24 [28: 28: 32: 32: 34: 34: 36: 38] sts, and patt to end.

Complete to match first side, reversing shapings.

FRONT

Work same as Back.

SLEEVES

Using 3.5mm (US 4) needles, cast on 68 [68: 68: 68: 76: 76: 76: 84: 84] sts.

Row 1 (RS): K3, *P2, K2; rep from * to last 5 sts, P2, K3.

Row 2 (WS): P3, *K2, P2; rep from * to last 5 sts, K2, P3.

Last 2 rows set pattern.

Cont in K2, P2 Rib as set for 10cm from beg, ending with RS facing for next row. Place a marker each side of the centre 2 sts. 33 [33: 33: 33: 37: 37: 37: 41: 41] sts each side.

Beg diagonal rib shaping

Row 1 (RS): K1, M1K, pm, patt to 2 sts before first marker, P2tog, sm, K2, sm, P2tog, patt to last st, pm, M1K, k1.

Row 2 (Inc–WS): P1, M1P, P to next marker, sm, patt to next marker, sm, P2, sm, patt to next marker, sm, P to last st, M1P, P1—2 sts inc'd. 70 [70: 70: 70: 78: 78: 78: 86: 86] sts.

Note: Inc'd sts at each side edge are worked into st st, whilst the K2, P2 rib sts are decreased each side of the centre 2 sts.

Rows 3 and 5: K1, M1K, K to first marker, sm, patt to 2 sts before next marker, SKP, sm, K2, sm, K2tog, patt to last marker, sm, K to last st, M1K, k1.

Rows 4 and 6 (WS): P to next marker, sm, patt to next marker, sm, P2, sm, patt to next marker, sm, P to end.

Row 7: Rep row 1.

Row 8 (Inc–WS): Rep row 2—2 sts inc'd. 72 [72: 72: 72: 80: 80: 80: 88: 88] sts.

These 8 rows set pat for *centre dec only with no change in number of sts, and the WS rows are worked as K the knit sts and P the purl sts, except for the inc rows.*

Rep these 8 rows 5 times more, BUT only work an inc row **every foll 6th row.** 84 [84: 84: 84: 92: 92: 92: 100: 100] sts. Sleeve should meas approx. 25cm from beg, ending with RS facing for next row

Discontinue rib and work all sts in st st, working increases as foll:

Next row (RS): K1, M1K, knit to last st, M1K, k1. 86 [86: 86: 86: 94: 94: 94: 102: 102] sts.

Cont to inc 1 st each side every foll 8th [4th: 4th: 4th: 4th: 4th: 4th: 4th: 4th] row 6 [2: 5: 11: 11: 13: 12: 14: 12] times more, then every foll 0 [6th: 6th: 6th: 6th: 2nd: 2nd: 0: 2nd] row 0 [8: 6: 2: 2: 2: 4: 0: 4] times. 98 [106: 108: 112: 120: 124: 126: 130: 134] sts.

Cont straight, if necessary, until sleeve meas 45cm from beg, ending with RS facing for next row.

Shape raglan sleeve cap

Dec row 1 (RS): K2, SKP, knit to last 4 sts, K2tog, K2. 96 [104: 106: 110: 118: 122: 124: 128: 132] sts.

Row 2 (WS): Purl.

Rep these 2 rows 21 [21: 26: 28: 28: 28: 33: 31: 33] times more. 54 [62: 54: 54: 62: 66: 58: 66: 66] sts.

Next row (RS): Rep Dec row 1. 52 [60: 52: 52: 60: 64: 56: 64: 64] sts.

Next rows (WS): P2, P2tog, purl to last 4 sts, SPP, P2. 50 [58: 50: 50: 58: 62: 54: 62: 62] sts.

Rep these 2 rows 7 [9: 7: 7: 9: 10: 8: 10: 10] times more.

Cast off rem 22 sts.

MAKING UP

Block as described on information page.

Join sleeves using the set-in sleeve method instructions on information page.

Join side seams, leaving 10cm from cast-on edge unsewn for side splits.

Join sleeve seams.

High Neck

With RS facing and using 3.5mm (US 4) circular needle, beg at right back shoulder, pick up and K20 sts along shaped back neck edge, 24 [28: 28: 32: 32: 34: 34: 36: 38] sts along centre cast-off sts and 20 sts along left back neck edge, pick up in same way along front neck edge. 128 [136: 136: 144: 144: 148: 148: 152: 156] sts. Join to work in rounds.

Next rnd: *K2, P2; rep from * around.

This rnd sets patt.

Work in patt for 10cm. Cast off sts loosely in patt.

INFORMATION

TENSION

Obtaining the correct tension is perhaps the single factor that can make the difference between a successful garment and a disastrous one. It controls both the shape and size of an article, so any variation, however slight, can distort the finished garment. Different designers feature in our books, and it is their tension, given at the start of each pattern, which you must match. We recommend that you knit a square in pattern and/or stocking stitch (depending on the pattern instructions) of perhaps 5 - 10 more stitches and 5 - 10 more rows than those given in the tension note. Mark out the central 10cm square with pins. If you have too many stitches to 10cm, try again using thicker needles, if you have too few stitches to 10cm, try again using finer needles. Once you have achieved the correct tension your garment will be knitted to the measurements indicated in the size diagram shown at the end of the pattern.

CHART NOTE

Many of the patterns in the book are worked from charts. Each square on a chart represents a stitch and each line of squares a row of knitting. Each colour used is given a different letter and these are shown in the materials section, or in the key alongside the chart of each pattern. When working from the charts, read odd rows (K) from right to left and even rows (P) from left to right, unless otherwise stated. When working lace from a chart it is important to note that all but the largest size may have to alter the first and last few stitches in order not to lose or gain stitches over the row.

WORKING A LACE PATTERN

When working a lace pattern, it is important to remember that if you are unable to work both the increase and corresponding decrease and vice versa, the stitches should be worked in stocking stitch.

KNITTING WITH COLOUR

There are two main methods of working colour into a knitted fabric: **Intarsia** and **Fairisle** techniques. The first method produces a single thickness of fabric and is usually used where a colour is only required in a particular area of a row and does not form a repeating pattern across the row, as in the fairisle technique.

Fairisle type knitting: When two or three colours are worked repeatedly across a row, strand the yarn not in use loosely behind the stitches being worked. If you are working with more than two colours, treat the "floating" yarns as if they were one yarn and always spread the stitches to their correct width to keep them elastic. It is advisable not to carry the stranded or "floating" yarns over more than three stitches at a time, but to weave them under and over the colour you are working. The "floating" yarns are therefore caught at the back of the work.

Intarsia: The simplest way to do this is to cut short lengths of yarn for each motif or block of colour used in a row. Then, joining in the various colours at the appropriate point on the row, link one colour to the next by twisting them around each other where they meet on the wrong side to avoid gaps. All ends can then either be darned along the colour join lines, as each motif is completed or can be "knitted-in" to the fabric of the knitting as each colour is worked into the pattern. This is done in much the same way as "weaving-in" yarns when working the Fairisle technique and does save time darning-in ends. It is essential that the tension is noted for intarsia as this may vary from the stocking stitch if both are used in the same pattern.

FINISHING INSTRUCTIONS

After working for hours knitting a garment, it seems a great pity that many garments are spoiled because such little care is taken in the pressing and finishing process. Follow the text below for a truly professional-looking garment.

PRESSING

Block out each piece of knitting and following the instructions on the ball band, press the garment pieces, omitting the ribs. Tip: Take special care to press the edges, as this will make sewing up both easier and neater. If the ball band indicates that the fabric is not to be pressed, then covering the blocked out fabric with a damp white cotton cloth and leaving it to stand will have the desired effect. Darn in all ends neatly along the selvedge edge or a colour join, as appropriate.

STITCHING

When stitching the pieces together, remember to match areas of colour and texture very carefully where they meet. Use a seam stitch such as mattress stitch or back stitch for all main knitting seams and join all ribs and neckband with mattress stitch, unless otherwise stated.

CONSTRUCTION

Having completed the pattern instructions, join the left shoulder and neckband seams as detailed above. Sew the top of the sleeve to the body of the garment using the method detailed in the pattern, referring to the appropriate guide:

Straight cast-off sleeves: Place centre of cast-off edge of sleeve to shoulder seam. Sew top of sleeve to body, using markers as guidelines where applicable.

Square set-in sleeves: Place centre of cast-off edge of sleeve to shoulder seam. Set sleeve head into armhole, the straight sides at top of sleeve to form a neat right-angle to cast-off sts at armhole on back and front.

Shallow set-in sleeves: Place centre of cast off edge of sleeve to shoulder seam. Match decreases at beg of armhole shaping to decreases at top of sleeve. Sew sleeve head into armhole, easing in shapings.

Set-in sleeves: Place centre of cast-off edge of sleeve to shoulder seam. Set in sleeve, easing sleeve head into armhole.
Join side and sleeve seams.
Slip stitch pocket edgings and linings into place.
Sew on buttons to correspond with buttonholes.
Ribbed welts and neckbands and any areas of garter stitch should not be pressed.
Wash as directed on the ball band.

ABBREVIATIONS

K	knit
P	purl
st(s)	stitch(es)
inc	increas(e)(ing)
dec	decreas(e)(ing)
st st	stocking stitch (1 row K, 1 row P)
g st	garter stitch (K every row)
beg	begin(ning)
foll	following
rem	remain(ing)
rev st st	reverse stocking stitch (1 row K , 1 row P)
rep	repeat
rnd	round
alt	alternate
cont	continue
patt	pattern
tog	together
mm	millimetres
cm	centimetres
in(s)	inch(es)
RS	right side
WS	wrong side
sl 1	slip one stitch
psso	pass slipped stitch over
p2sso	pass 2 slipped stitches over
tbl	through back of loop
M1	make one stitch by picking up horizontal loop before next stitch and knitting into back of it
M1P	make one stitch by picking up horizontal loop before next stitch and purling into back of it
yfwd	yarn forward
yrn	yarn round needle
meas	measures
0	no stitches, times or rows
-	no stitches, times or rows for that size
yon	yarn over needle
yfrn	yarn forward round needle
wyib	with yarn at back
wyif	with yarn at front

BUTTONS, BEADS & RIBBON

Bedecked Haberdashery
The Coach House
Barningham Park
Richmond
North Yorkshire
DL11 7DW

TEL: +44 (0) 1833 621 451
eMail: thegirls@bedecked.co.uk **Web:** www.bedecked.co.uk

EXPERIENCE RATING
(for guidance only)

● Beginner Techniques
For the beginner knitter, basic garment shaping and straight forward stitch technique.

●● Simple Techniques
Simple straight forward knitting, introducing various shaping techniques and garments.

●●● Experienced Techniques
For the more experienced knitter, using more advanced shaping techniques at the same time as colourwork or different stitch techniques.

●●●● Advanced Techniques
Advanced techniques used, using advanced stitches and garment shapings.

WASH CARE INFORMATION
You may have noticed over the last season that the wash care symbols on our ball bands and shade cards have changed. This is to bring the symbols we use up to date and hopefully help you to care for your knitting and crochet more easily. Below are the symbols you are likely to see and a brief explanation of each.

MACHINE WASH SYMBOLS

HAND WASH SYMBOLS

DRY CLEAN SYMBOLS

IRONING SYMBOLS

DO NOT BLEACH SYMBOL

DRYING SYMBOLS

SIZING GUIDE

When you knit and wear a Rowan design, we want you to look and feel fabulous. This all starts with the size and fit of the design you choose. We have recently increased our size range to help you achieve the best fit for your knitwear. Our womenswear sizes now range from 28"/71cm through to 62"/157cm chest.

Dimensions in the charts below are body measurements, not garment dimensions; therefore please refer to the measuring guide to help you to determine which is the best size for you to knit.

....

STANDARD SIZING GUIDE FOR WOMEN

....

The sizing within this chart is based on the larger size within the range.

To fit bust

28-30	32–34	36–38	40–42	44–46	48–50	52-54	56-58	60-62	inches
71–76	81–86	91–97	102–107	112–117	122–127	132-137	142-147	152-157	cm

To fit waist

20-22	24–26	28–30	32–34	36–38	40–42	44–46	48–50	52-54	inches
51-56	61–66	71–76	81–86	91–97	102–107	112-117	122-127	132-137	cm

To fit hips

30-31	34–36	38–40	42–44	46–48	50–52	54-56	58-60	62-64	inches
76-81	86–91	97–102	107–112	117–122	127–132	137-142	147-152	157-162	cm

Bust .....
Waist ....
Hips .....

SIZING DIAGRAM NOTE

The instructions are given for the smallest size. Where they vary, work the figures in brackets for the larger sizes. One set of figures refers to all sizes.

Included with most patterns is a size diagram, see image below of the finished garment and its dimensions. The measurement shown at the bottom of each size diagram shows the garment width. The size diagram will also indicate how the garment is constructed — for example, if the garment has a drop shoulder, this will be reflected in the drawing.

To help you choose the size of garment to knit, please refer to the sizing guide. Generally, in the majority of designs, the welt width (at the cast-on edge of the garment) is the same width as the chest.

If you don't want to measure yourself, note the size of a similar shaped garment that you own and compare it with the size diagram given at the end of the pattern.

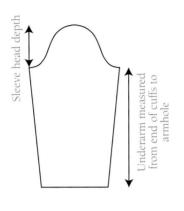
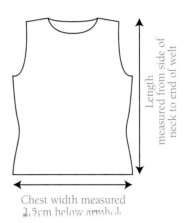

Chest width measured
2.5cm below armhole

MEASURING GUIDE

For maximum comfort and to ensure the correct fit when choosing a size to knit, please follow the tips below when checking your size. Measure yourself close to your body, over your underwear and don't pull the tape measure too tight!

Bust/chest | measure around the fullest part of the bust/chest and across the shoulder blades.

Waist | measure around the natural waistline, just above the hip bones.

Hips | measure around the fullest part of the bottom.

Finally, once you have decided which size is best for you, please ensure that you achieve the tension required for the design you wish to knit.

Remember, if your tension is too loose, your garment will be bigger than the pattern size and you may use more yarn. If your tension is too tight, your garment could be smaller than the pattern size and you will have yarn left over.

Furthermore, if your tension is incorrect, the handle of your fabric will be too stiff or floppy and will not fit properly. It really does make sense to check your tension before starting every project.

MODEL SIZE INFORMATION

Model (Amy) wears a UK dress size 10, height 5ft 9in, bust 32–34in

All of the photography garments were knitted in the following bust size: 32-34in

DISTRIBUTORS

AUSTRALIA: Morris and Sons
Level 1, 234 Collins Street, Melbourne Vic 3000
Tel: 03 9654 0888   **Web:** morrisandsons.com.au

AUSTRALIA: Morris and Sons
50 York Street, Sydney NSW 2000
Tel: 02 92998588   **Web:** morrisandsons.com.au

AUSTRIA: DMC
5 Avenue de Suisse BP 189, Illzach (France)
Email: info-FR@dmc.com

BELGIUM: DMC
5 Avenue de Suisse BP 189, Illzach (France)
Email: info-FR@dmc.com

CANADA: Sirdar USA Inc.
406 20th Street SE, Hickory, North Carolina, USA 28602
Tel: 828 404 3705   **Email:** sirdarusa@sirdar.co.uk

CHINA: Commercial Agent Mr Victor Li,
Email: victor.li@mezcrafts.com

CHINA: Shanghai Yujun CO.LTD.
Room 701 Wangjiao Plaza, No.175 Yan'an Road, 200002 Shanghai, China
Tel: +86 2163739785 **Email:** jessechang@vip.163.com

DENMARK: Carl J. Permin A/S
Egegaardsvej 28 DK-2610 Rødovre
Tel: (45) 36 36 89 89 **Email:** permin@permin.dk
Web: www.permin.dk

ESTONIA: Mez Crafts Estonia OÜ
Helgi tee 2, Peetri alevik, Tallinn, 75312 Harjumaa
Tel: +372 6 306 759 **Email:** info.ee@mezcrafts.com
Web: www.mezcrafts.ee

FINLAND: Prym Consumer Finland Oy
Huhtimontie 6, 04200 KERAVA
Tel: +358 9 274871 **Email:** sales.fi@prym.com

FRANCE: DMC
5 Avenue de Suisse BP 189, Illzach (France)
Email: info-FR@dmc.com

GERMANY: DMC
5 Avenue de Suisse BP 189, Illzach (France)
Email: info-DE@dmc.com

HOLLAND: G. Brouwer & Zn B.V.
Oudhuijzerweg 69, 3648 AB Wilnis
Tel: 0031 (0) 297-281 557 **Email:** info@gbrouwer.nl

ICELAND: Carl J. Permin A/S
Egegaardsvej 28, DK-2610 Rødovre
Tel: (45) 36 72 12 00 **Email:** permin@permin.dk
Web: www.permin.dk

ITALY: DMC
Via Magenta 77/5, Rho (Milano)
Email: info-IT@dmc.com

JAPAN: DMC KK
Santo Building 7F,13, Kanda Konya Cho, Chiyodaku, 101-0035, Tokyo
Email: ouchi@dmc-kk.com

KOREA: My Knit Studio
3F, 59 Insadong-gil, Jongno-gu, 03145, Seoul
Tel: 82-2-722-0006 **Email:** myknit@myknit.com
Web: www.myknit.com

LATVIA: Latvian Crafts
12-2, Jurģu street, LV-2011
Tel: +371 37 126326825 **Email:** vjelkins@latviancrafts.lv
Web: www.latviancrafts.lv

LEBANON: y.knot
Saifi Village, Mkhalissiya Street 162, Beirut
Tel: (961) 1 992211 **Email:** y.knot@cyberia.net.lb

LUXEMBOURG: DMC
5 Avenue de Suisse BP 189, Illzach (France)
Email: info-FR@dmc.com

NEW ZEALAND: Trendy Trims
7 Angle Street, Onehunga, Auckland, New Zealand
Email: trendy@trendytrims.co.nz **Web:** trendytrims.co.nz

NORWAY: Carl J. Permin A/S
Andersrudveien 1, 1914, Ytre Enebakk
Tel: 23 16 35 30 **Email:** permin@permin.dk
Web: www.permin.dk

PORTUGAL: DMC
P. Ferrocarriles Catalanes, 117 oficina 34, Cornellá de llobregat, 08940
Email: info-PT @dmc.com

RUSSIA: Family Hobby
Zelenograd, Haus 1505, Raum III, 124683
Email: tv@fhobby.ru **Web:** www.family-hobby.ru

SOUTH AFRICA: Arthur Bales LTD
62 4th Avenue, Linden 2195
Tel: (27) 11 888 2401 **Email:** info@arthurbales.co.za
Web: www.arthurbales.co.za

SPAIN: DMC
P. Ferrocarriles Catalanes, 117 oficina 34, Cornellá de llobregat, 08940
Email: info-SP @dmc.com

SWEDEN: Carl J. Permin A/S
Skaraborgsvägen 35C, 3tr, Borås
Tel: 33 12 77 10 **Email:** sverige@permin.dk
Web: www.permin.dk

SWITZERLAND: DMC
5 Avenue de Suisse BP 189, Illzach (France)
Email: info-DE@dmc.com

USA.: Sirdar USA Inc
406 20th Street SE, Hickory, North Carolina, USA 28602
Tel: 828 404 3705 **Email:** sirdarusa@sirdar.co.uk
Web: www.sirdar.com

UK: Rowan
Flanshaw Lane, Alverthorpe, Wakefield, WF2 9ND, United Kingdom
Tel: 01924 371501 **Email:** mail@knitrowan.com

For more stockists in all countries please visit **www.knitrowan.com**